THE LITTLE BOOK OF
CALM
AT
WORK

PAUL WILSON

PENGUIN BOOKS

PENGUIN BOOKS

Published by the Penguin Group
Penguin Books Ltd, 80 Strand, London WC2R 0RL, England
Penguin Putnam Inc., 375 Hudson Street, New York, New York 10014, USA
Penguin Books Australia Ltd, 250 Camberwell Road, Camberwell, Victoria 3124, Australia
Penguin Books Canada Ltd, 10 Alcorn Avenue, Toronto, Ontario, Canada M4V 3B2
Penguin Books India (P) Ltd, 11 Community Centre, Panchsheel Park, New Delhi – 110 017, India
Penguin Books (NZ) Ltd, Cnr Rosedale and Airborne Roads, Albany, Auckland, New Zealand
Penguin Books (South Africa) (Pty) Ltd, 24 Sturdee Avenue, Rosebank 2196, South Africa

Penguin Books Ltd, Registered Offices: 80 Strand, London WC2R 0RL, England
www.penguin.com

First published 1998
8 10 12 14 16 15 13 11 9

Copyright © The Calm Centre Pty Ltd, 1998
All rights reserved

The moral right of the author has been asserted

Set in Monotype Phaistos
Printed in England by William Clowes Ltd

Oh yes, we can all feel calm on the weekend. Carefree, relaxed, easygoing. It's those other five days that put us to the test. The five days we work.

But how would you feel if every day could be like the weekend?

It's easy.

That's what The Little Book of Calm at Work *is all about.*

Let this book fall open to any page for the suggestion that will work best for you at this particular moment on this particular day. Take it on face value. Let your subconscious run with it.

And please don't take it too seriously – being calm is meant to be enjoyed!

Conquer all workplace tensions with
Paul Wilson's complete work,
Calm at Work.

'His jargon-free, no-nonsense ideas
are remarkably simple.'
Evening Standard

TAKE THE FIRST STEP

The most important step in becoming
calm at work – one that will have you
heading down that path in no time at
all – is simply making the decision to
do something about becoming calm.
Make the decision now.

ACT CALM

When you pretend you are calm, and
adopt the characteristics of a calm
person, you'll convince yourself you're
calm in no time.

GO BONSAI

Sometimes, even the smallest glimpse of
nature is all you need to escape the
pressures of everyday life. Bonsai can
bring a 'meditation garden' experience
into your home or office.

CARRY A NOTEBOOK

Two of the most powerful tools for
overcoming the stresses of a busy life
are a pen and notepad. Write down
your worries and watch them diminish.
Write down what you are going to
achieve in your day, and watch your
tasks fall into order.

ADMIT YOUR IGNORANCE

The faster you admit to not having
the answer to something, the more time
you have to find one.

BE RUTHLESS WITH PAPER

Rid yourself of the burden and
distraction of non-essential information
by using the wastepaper
basket – ruthlessly.

SEPARATE MAJOR FROM MINOR

You can add harmony to your day
simply by dividing your day into 'big
picture' times, and 'small picture'
(detail) times. The less they overlap,
the calmer you will remain.

KEEP IT SIMPLE

The more complex your life and work,
the more stressful they are inclined to
become. Search for the simple course,
and you'll find things run smoother.

WORRY WHEN THE TIME COMES

Worry always relates to the future. So if you devote your full attention to what is going on now, not only will you feel calmer, but the future will take care of itself.

REHEARSE YOUR CLEVERNESS

If you put as much thought into the communication of your work efforts as you do into their formulation, you will overcome the most common of workplace frustrations: being misunderstood or ignored.

GO PARKING

Just a few minutes wandering through a
leafy park or garden — even in the heart
of the city — is a shortcut to balance
and tranquillity.

SPACE YOUR ENGAGEMENTS

Allow a fifteen-minute buffer zone between each appointment. Not only does it enrich your day with stress-free space, it improves the quality of your engagements.

SQUEEZE BALLS

Squeezing a ball will help work off the
nervous tension that concentrates in
your fingers and hands.

DO THE TYPE-A SIDESTEP

If you have too many Type-A (driven, competitive, tense) personality traits, avoid other Type-As as much as practicality and decency permits.

DO IT OVER AND OVER AGAIN

You can make a calming and meditative exercise out of any repetitive task or action if you concentrate on it, to the exclusion of all else, for an extended period of time.

TAKE THE EASY WAY OUT

Being calm is, in itself, one of life's
great pleasures. Finding calm should be
a pleasure, too.

INDULGE YOUR BODY

One of the most effective ways
to maintain a state of calm is also one
of the most pleasurable. Regular
massage is as good for the soul as it
is for the body.

BE CLEAR WITH AMBITION

When ambition is coupled with unclear
goals, you have a stressful combination.
Make it your ambition to stay calm
with clear goals and objectives.

TAKE FUN SERIOUSLY

Your job doesn't have to be all
hard work. With a little bit of effort
in changing the way you look at it,
even the most serious occupations
can be fun.

SCHEDULE ONE HOUR

Create peace and order in your life by
scheduling at least one hour of
unscheduled time – just for yourself –
in your day.

FIND PEACE IN A VASE

Nature has a way of healing
everything . . . especially feelings of
stress and tension. For the non-
allergic, a vase of colourful flowers —
or a flowering pot plant — can keep you
in touch with this power.

HAVE A MINUTE OF STILL

From time to time throughout your day,
concentrate on becoming still — on
slowing your breathing, limiting your
movements, stilling your thoughts.
From stillness comes peace.

COUNTER A FLUORO

Electric lights, television, computers,
and fluorescent lights all add to feelings
of tension. Paradoxically, you can
compensate for them with another
electronic implement – a negative ion
generator, or ioniser.

KNOW WHAT'S IMPORTANT

Decide what is important in your life –
money, position, success, family,
relationships – and prioritise your
worklife accordingly. Then you won't
lose sleep over the unimportant things
in your working day.

FIND SERENITY IN ORDER

Disorganisation is the opposite
to calm – it creates chaos, demands
attention, and constantly reminds you
of all that remains to be done. Creating
order gives you the space to
become calm.

TAKE THE UNCONSCIOUS ROUTE

If you tell your subconscious what you want, then trust it to deliver, it will become your best planning resource, your best source of creativity, and your best route to calm.

RETIRE EARLY

It's true what mother told you: an hour's sleep before midnight is worth two after.

BACK UP RELIGIOUSLY

To always feel calm about using your computer, make a rigorous routine of backing up your work.

USE YOUR CHILDREN'S EYES

Try to view the more serious aspects of
life through a child's eyes. See, it
doesn't look so serious now, does it?

ROLL WITH THE PUNCHES

In many martial arts, the aim is to
turn the force of your opponent to your
own advantage. This is also true of
remaining calm in the workplace.
Go with the flow. Use it to
your advantage.

TURN DOWN SUCCESS

Contrary to what you've been taught
since childhood, it is not essential that
you succeed in everything you do. Some
people stay calm by walking away
from 'success'.

CHAT ABOUT CALM

One of the extraordinary side-effects
of speaking about 'calm' is that it
induces feelings of calm. Now you
know what to talk about next time
you're feeling tense.

Turn to C

Choose to eat more foods rich
in vitamin C – most fruits and
vegetables – because they have a
positive effect on your mental health
and help you remain calm.

Shrug

You'll feel calm if you walk away from
the things you can't do anything about,
and concentrate on those you can
influence.

SEIZE THE MOMENT

When you concentrate wholly on
whatever you have to do – however
mundane or meaningless it may appear –
time flies, you derive satisfaction from
your efforts, and you're well on the
way to becoming calm and relaxed.

SNATCH A COUPLE OF MINUTES

When you take brief cat naps throughout the day, you'll be surprised at how much peace you can derive from just a couple of minutes — even while sitting at your desk.

STOP TO SMELL THE ROSES

Certain scents stimulate the production
of the relaxing chemical, serotonin, in
the brain. Among the more effective
of these scents are lavender
and chamomile.

LOOK FOR A SIGN

You can easily overcome rising tension
as long as you are aware of its
approach. Look for the signs — such as
when your speech speeds up, or your
breathing becomes shallow — as a signal
that it's time to concentrate on
becoming calm.

PLANT YOUR EQUIPMENT

A single plant – or several of them – is
the natural way to counter the restless
electronic outputs of photocopiers,
lights and computer monitors.

TALK YOURSELF INTO IT

To become calm, say to yourself, 'Each
moment I feel more peace and calm
envelop me. I spread this feeling to all
I come in contact with.' Say it slowly,
with as much certainty as possible.

EXAGGERATE YOUR HEIGHT

Imagine your body being suspended
only centimetres above the ground. Feel
it lift. A lightness will overtake your
entire body.

TAKE YOUR TIME

Contrary to what you may tell yourself,
you have all the time in the world to do
whatever you choose. What cannot be
fitted into your day, cannot be done —
forget about it.

TURN ON TO WATER

Drink *lots* more water than you think
you need and not only will you have
better health, you will have increased
feelings of calm.

CALL IT A DAY

At the end of every workday, give
yourself permission to have the rest
of the day off – to relax and indulge
yourself. It might sound obvious, but
so few do it.

GO TO THE CENTRE

You often hear of athletes and actors 'centering' themselves before a performance. You can do the same – to become calm and more effective – just by concentrating on the ebb and flow of your own breath.

REPLAY CALM MOMENTS

Recall one calm experience from more relaxing times. Luxuriate in that experience. Every time you need to relax, simply revisit that moment.

GET YOUR KICKS OUT OF CALM

While stimulants may have their place,
it's certainly not for becoming calm.
Substitute exercise, herbal teas, and
healthy foods for their more stimulating
counterparts — and find the pleasure in
becoming calm.

SKIP ALL DEADLINES

When someone issues you with a
deadline, immediately translate it into
an amount of time you can utilise
however you choose – then you will
be calling the shots rather than
someone else.

FILL THE MOMENT WITH LIFE

Life is at its richest, and is most
fulfilling and productive, when you
approach it with enthusiasm.

WORK ON YOUR
GREENGROCER

Choose fruit in preference to tension-
building snack foods, and you'll remain
more relaxed throughout your day.

BREATHE EASILY

Deep, slow breathing is at the root of
all great achievements in martial arts,
theatre and relaxation. Breathe deeply
and slowly, listening to each breath as
it comes and goes . . . and you'll
become calm.

MAKE YOUR FRIENDS WORK

There are no prizes for being miserable
alone. The weight will begin to lift the
moment you share your problems with
those who are close to you. That's what
friends are for.

PACE IT OUT

When tensions rise, when your
problems start to get you down,
drop what you're doing and start to
pace. Quickly.

DECLINE POLITELY

Knowing when to decline additional
work or social activities is often the
difference between performing well and
being over-extended.

SEEK THE UPSIDE

It is not always easy to see the positive
and optimistic side of the events in
your life. But if you take the trouble to
search, your creativity will reveal them
over and over again.

MAKE PEACE

Why should you carry the weight of
regret or ill will? Make peace quickly
and you'll be well on the way to
becoming calm again.

RAISE A FEW EYEBROWS

A simple way to relieve the tension
that gathers in the face and brow is to
adopt a 'surprised look' – slightly
raised eyebrows, slightly turned up
corners of the mouth.

APPRECIATE SILENCE

If you consider that silence is not so much an absence of sound as a presence of peace, you will soon learn to appreciate this beautiful state.

LOOK FOR LITTLE COMFORTS

Comfort is one of the key elements
of being calm – comfortable
temperatures, comfortable seating,
comfortable clothing.

CAN THE COFFEE

Despite the leisurely atmosphere it is often consumed in, coffee adds to your tension levels – for hours after you've consumed it. Find a caffeine-free substitute, and become calm.

TAKE OFF EARLY

Set out several minutes before you
have to and you'll find yourself
either relaxed and on time, or with
relaxing time to spare before your
next engagement.

DINE LIGHTLY

Light foods, raw foods and easily-digested foods are those that have become known as 'calm foods'. Choose them, not just because they're good for you, but because they make you feel good.

WAIT FOR THE AGENDA

If you want to stay calm, never go
into a meeting unless it has a clearly
defined outcome.

FEEL YOUR PULSE

Listen to the sound of your pulse as
you slow your breathing. Repeat to
yourself, over and over again, 'My
pulse is calm and regular.' Before you
know it, you will be calm.

BE THANKFUL FOR THE BURDEN

Those who have heavy workloads invariably feel more secure in their jobs than those who have little to do.

STEAL A CALM HIDEAWAY

Find yourself a special place – a chair,
a room, a corner – that you can
associate with feelings of being calm
and relaxed. Go there, and sit quietly,
whenever the need arises.

BARE IT

The first thing you do when you decide
to relax is kick off your shoes. So kick
them off and calm down now.

PLAN

When you know where you're going,
you'll find it easier to stay calm on the
way there. Plan, and become calm.

GET IT REGULARLY

Regular exercise helps you to cope
better, and will leave you feeling more
calm and contented.

KNOW YOUR LIMITS

There is only so much you are capable
of handling or achieving at any given
time. Recognise your limits, and you'll
be more relaxed about what you do.

SET YOUR OWN
BENCHMARKS

One of the greatest strains in life is
having to live up to the standards
others set for us. For your own
efficiency and state of mind, convert
other people's benchmarks into
your own.

SAVE PERFECTION FOR OTHERS

If you leave perfection for others, and simply work to the best of your ability most of the time, calm and satisfaction will surely follow.

FORSAKE THE ROUTINE

Many stresses are habitual. So stepping
outside of your routine, and taking on a
new activity – several times a day –
will steer you on a course to calm.

RELAX ON THE OTHER SIDE
OF THE GOALS

The steps along the way to achievement
become more satisfying when you
reward yourself for goals and
targets realised.

MAKE CHANGE FOR THE BETTER

You can be calm about change if you embrace it, and strive to make it lead to better things.

BLEND

Social interaction is a cheap and
cheerful way to overcome the
stresses that arise from loneliness
or insularity. To become calm, mix
without expectation.

PLAY WITH YOURSELF

Your subconscious will help you feel
calm and at peace if you play games
with it: have fun, pretend, appeal to the
imagination rather than the intellect.

CULTIVATE A COOL LOOK

You can be well on the way to calm just
by adopting the superficial
characteristics of a calm person —
easy stance, relaxed jaw, smiling face
and unclenched fingers.

STROKE YOUR BROW

During a hard day, tension gathers in
the facial area. To find relief from this,
drag your fingertips – pressing firmly –
from your forehead to the back of
your head.

USE AN AIR FRESHENER

Whether it's wide open space in the outdoors, or a chair placed by an open window, fresh air is one of the most powerful counterbalances to stress and anxiety.

ASSUME YOU'RE IN CONTROL

It's amazing how easy it is to trick your subconscious into believing you're in control of what you do, just by acting as if you are in control of what you do.

LOOK AHEAD A YEAR AGO

If you want to put today's problems and
worries into perspective, imagine how
important they will seem if you look
back in a year's time.

GIVE TENSION THE FINGER

There's a relaxing acupressure point at
either side of the bridge of your nose.
Rub there gently, and around your eyes,
and feel the tension dissolve.

LOOK OUT FOR A LAUGH

You can't feel bad when you're
feeling good.

LEAN ON A TREE

There's a calmness about trees. Choose one that's a pleasure to be near, then use it as a place to visit whenever you feel pressured.

CHEW SLOWLY

When you chew each bite slowly, not only do you make your refection more refreshing, it becomes more relaxing as you eat. This is particularly so in fast-paced work environments.

FIND CALM IN SPACE

You'll find it easier to feel calm in the
centre of a room rather than the corner;
away from the crowd rather than in the
midst; in the park rather than in the
elevator. Create the impression of
space, and you'll find calm.

CONTEMPLATE YOUR NAVEL

When you take a deep breath your
diaphragm swells and you'll feel your
tummy rise near your navel. Be aware
of this sensation throughout your day
and you'll find it easy to relax.

GO TO WORK ON A KIWI

Foods high in potassium, such as
kiwi fruit and bananas, are often
associated with feelings of wellbeing
and cheerfulness.

GET TO THE POINT

In the workplace, there is no substitute
for knowing what you want, and asking
for it as directly as you can. Plan,
rehearse and be assertive, and you'll
feel in control of what you're doing.

CONSORT WITH THE CALM

Calm is catching. Enjoy being
around calm people — not for the
stimulation, but for the peaceful
feelings they spread.

LET OTHERS SUCCEED

The greatest time and sanity saver in
the workplace is delegation. The key to
doing it successfully is to focus on the
things that you are best at, and to hand
over everything else – the
responsibility as well as
the workload.

ASK AND YOU SHALL RECEIVE

It's remarkable how much you can achieve in the workplace by simply asking for what you want rather than waiting for it to be offered.

AVOID QUEUES

Often, the only calm place in a queue is
at the front. Phone, fax or write –
anything to avoid queuing. And if you
can't avoid it, allow twice as much time
as you think you need to get to
the head.

DIP YOUR LIDS

You can create a moment of calm for
yourself simply by lowering your
eyelids – slowly. If you concentrate on
allowing the muscles in your face to
relax at the same time, your calm will
be enhanced.

DEAL WITH THAT PROBLEM

Action overcomes the stressful nature
of procrastination. Deal with each
problem as it arises, and you will have
cleared the way to peace of mind.

DO YOUR HOMEWORK

In any competitive environment, the more you know about what is going on, the more secure you will feel about it. Study, prepare, know your topic – then you have the resources to remain calm.

HAVE A LIFE

Contrary to what the boss might have you believe, there *is* more to life than work. Maintain the balance and you can maintain a sense of calm.

VARY THE PATTERN

When you find yourself under pressure,
do something different. Work in a way
you wouldn't normally work, think a
way you wouldn't normally think, sit in
someone else's chair.

GO EASY ON YOURSELF

Many find the greatest pressures in the
workplace are self-imposed. Be
reasonable with the ambitions,
schedules and deadlines you create for
yourself, and you'll leave yourself room
to become calm.

MOVE ON

Funny thing about humans is the way
they love to dwell on the past – what
they did, what they might have done,
what they should have done. Calm
people tell themselves that nothing they
do can change what's past . . . then they
get on with enjoying life.

HUSH THE PHONE

Alarming telephone rings are designed
to set your nerves on edge. If you can't
select a calming tone, at least turn the
volume down as low as possible.

WALK FOR TWENTY
MINUTES

Whenever you feel under pressure
or are suffering from anxiety, take to
the street. Walk briskly for twenty
minutes – shoulders back, head held
high – and relaxation will follow.

ACE YOUR VITAMINS

Vitamins A, C, E and some of the B
group – the 'anti-oxidants' – are said
to have powerful healing, anti-ageing
and calming qualities.

CHOOSE YOUR BOSS

If you look at your job as you choosing
your boss, rather than your boss
choosing you, you'll always feel in
control of what you do.

FIND THE CALM SIDE OF TENSION

Note the contrast between 'tense' and 'relaxed' as you flex and unflex your muscles. Dwell on what 'relaxed' really feels like.

IMAGINE EVERY NINETY MINUTES

The human cycle of rest and efficiency requires a few minutes of right brain activity (creativity, imagination, visualisation, daydreaming) every ninety minutes. Make this switch regularly and you'll know how to remain calm.

SEARCH IN YOUR SPARE TIME

Instead of searching for distraction or stimulation, use your spare time to search for ways of becoming calm.

TAKE A COURSE

A sure way to break out of a stressful
work pattern is to take a self-
development course. Not only will you
have something new to focus on, you
can learn ways to achieve a fulfilling
and stress-free job.

LAUGH AT THE BOSS

If you'd like to feel more 'equal' to
those higher up than yourself, try
imagining them in ridiculous clothes or
guises. Once you have seen the
chairman as Mary Poppins, he will
never loom so threatening again.

SLOOOOOOW

Simply slowing down your movements, your speech patterns, or your rate of breathing works wonders in helping you achieve calm.

TRY TO BE GOOD

Altruism and acts of generosity can be
even more rewarding for the giver than
they are for the receiver. And when you
feel good, you'll feel calm.

Go slow

If you want to soothe a highly stressed colleague, consciously slow down your speech and gestures. Then you'll both end up calm.

CALM FROM MANY DIRECTIONS

By employing a number of little ways to calm throughout the day – rather than depending on one big calm hit – you'll find the path is made much smoother.

TAKE AN ANTIDOTE

Nature's instant antidote to tension is chamomile. Have a cup of chamomile tea – with a little honey or lemon if you prefer – when you want to relax.

DECIDE TO RELAX

Many times a day, give yourself
permission to relax. Give yourself
permission to forget your pressures and
concerns — for however brief a time —
and to become calm.

BREAK FOR A FACIAL

Nothing soaks away facial stress and
tension quite so pleasantly as a facial.
For something more immediate, try a
hot, damp face towel.

APPRECIATE CONFLICT

Those who are most calm about conflict
in the workplace are those who expect
it, accept it and treat it as a positive
part of communication.

STRIP

Loose, unrestricting garments are a shortcut to feeling physically relaxed. They even *look* relaxed.

ENJOY YOUR STRESS

Some stresses are good for us – a
rollercoaster ride, a pay rise, a brisk
walk up the stairs. Add some of this
positive stress to your day, and it will
help you remain calm.

CONCENTRATE ON ANYTHING

One of the core elements of meditation is concentration. You can still your thoughts by concentrating on any single thing – a task, an action, a sound, an image or concept. When your thoughts are still, you will be calm.

BE A LITTLE B

Easygoing personality types are
described as Type B. They're relaxed,
don't take life too seriously, and know
how to enjoy themselves. If you're not
this way inclined, *pretend* to be 'B' at
least once a day.

MOVE CALMLY

When you find yourself in a stressful
position, get up and move. Simply
moving away from your stressor is
often all it takes to become more
relaxed about it.

DO ZILCH

From time to time it's important to have nothing to do, and nothing on your agenda. Once you can be comfortable about being in this state, you can concentrate on becoming calm.

SKEW TO THE POSITIVE

Positive words have a positive impact
on your feelings. If you're creative
about substituting positive words or
thoughts for their more negative
counterparts, you can talk yourself into
becoming calm in no time.

CLINCH ONE BEFORE THE NEXT

Multi-tasking is something only computers can do efficiently. Complete each task before moving on to the next, and your increased efficiency will be matched only by your increased calm.

GET YOUR TEETH OUT

A smile produces instant stimulation of
the pleasure centre of your brain. Take
it a bit further, turn it into a laugh, and
the benefits are multiplied.

MAKE A CHOICE

Look for the choices in all aspects of
your work, and try to be aware of them
at all times. Then you'll always feel
you have some measure of control over
what happens.

STOP!

The first step to overcoming any stressful situation is to stop and reflect. Once you have considered your thoughts and your position, you can head towards becoming calm.

TUCK INTO HOLISM

A holistic approach to diet produces
calm as well as good health –
understandable when you know that
wholegrain flour, cereals and seeds are
rich in the 'stress fighters', vitamin B
and magnesium.

GET WORKLOAD INTO PERSPECTIVE

Your perception of workload usually relates to the amount of time you have at your disposal rather than the amount of work you have to do. Plan your time and your workload will take care of itself.

GO WILD

As wonderful and stimulating as the
modern world is, there is much to be
gained from getting away from it
occasionally. From time to time seek
peace and restoration in less
'civilised' places.

LEAVE OTHERS BE

If you concentrate on satisfying your
own obligations first – paying no heed
to anybody else's – you'll be more
calm, contented and efficient in what
you do.

LOOSEN THAT KNOT

Neckties can be more than a physical
restriction: they can be an emotional
and behavioural restriction as well.
Loosen that tie and give in to calm.

YOU SHOULD NEVER SAY SHOULD

Whenever you use 'should' in your thinking or conversation, you add pressure. Find a less demanding alternative, and life becomes more relaxing.

DIVIDE AND CONQUER

The stress of procrastination is easily
removed by dividing all big tasks into a
series of smaller ones, then taking on
the least pleasant ones first.

IMPROVE YOUR OWN CORNER

There's only one corner of the world you can be sure of improving – your own. If you strive to improve only the things you have the power to improve, you won't lose sleep over the impossible.

DECIDE TO BE ORGANISED

Set aside twenty minutes a day for
decision-making and organisation. Be
sure to make at least one decision
every time.

CREATE YOUR OWN CALM

Any act of creation — be it painting,
performing, sculpting, cooking — is as
calming as it is fulfilling.

TURN INSIDE

If you can turn off rationalism, and
tune into intuition, you'll have the best
possible guide to becoming calm.

ADJUST YOUR PICTURE

Form a mental picture of yourself –
calm, smiling and enthusiastic – and
refer back to it time and again
throughout the day.

KNUCKLE UNDER

All the relaxing acupressure points at
the bottom of your feet are easily
accessed by pressing your fist into
the sole of your foot. Press and
become calm.

HAVE SEX

Making love is good for your stress
levels as well as your soul.

MILLIONS WILL ENVY YOU

No matter what your circumstance
or position, millions would give
anything to be in that same position.
Strive to appreciate the positive aspects
of your life, and you'll become calmer
as a result.

GO BACK MANY YEARS

If yours was a pleasant childhood,
return there during times of stress
and tension. Relax in the comfort of
those memories.

HOLD YOUR CALLS

For many, the fewer telephone calls you make and take throughout a day, the more harmonious it seems.

GO GRACEFULLY

It is almost impossible to feel tense
when performing the simple, graceful
movements of a tai chi routine.

FLIGHT BEFORE FIGHT

When anger strikes, walk briskly for ten minutes, *then* have your say – so it's not only your emotion speaking.

DRESS UP YOUR FEARS

To take the sting out of your fears,
imagine yourself in a state of extreme
anxiety, then 'dress up' that mental
picture of yourself with something that
makes it amusing – silly clothes, face
paint, whatever. If it makes you smile,
all the better.

CULTIVATE A FRESH FETISH

Fresh air. Fresh fruit. Fresh flowers.
Wherever possible, add freshness to
your life, and find peace and beauty in
the process.

BE QUIET ONCE A DAY

Calm will be at hand if you spend time
in silence – at least fifteen minutes a
day – even if it means you have to rise
earlier to accommodate it.

KEEP AN EYE ON THE LIGHT

There's a light side to almost every situation — even those that, at first, may seem distressing. Look for this light side, have fun with it, and let it relax you all over.

CHANGE YOUR MIND

Resolve to change the way you think
about being able to remain calm.
Simply making that decision can be
enough to make you calm.

FORCE YOURSELF INTO CREATIVITY

There are three main forces in life –
creation, destruction and preservation.
Creation is the most positive. Strive
to find the most creative ways to live
your life and you'll find it easy to
remain calm.

ABOUT THE AUTHOR

Paul Wilson is known the world over as the guru of calm.

His first book, *The Calm Technique*, is considered one of the most influential in the genre. His second, the bestseller *Instant Calm*, has been translated into nineteen languages. His third major calm book, *Calm at Work*, is becoming even more popular.

However, it was his smallest book that won him the greatest acclaim. With sales of over 1,000,000, *The Little Book of Calm* spent more than twelve months at the top of the bestseller lists.

Now, with *The Little Book of Calm at Work*, the calm continues to spread.

Feel free to contact the author or share your calm at http://www.calmcentre.com

TURN WORK INTO A HOLIDAY

Imagine how relaxed you'd feel if you could add that easygoing, holiday feeling to every day of the week. All it takes is one little trigger — a photo, a momento, a Hawaiian shirt in your briefcase — and you're away!